LET'S GO HUNTING

Hunting RABBITS

Hines Lambert

I0877165

PowerKiDS press
New York

Published in 2013 by The Rosen Publishing Group, Inc.
29 East 21st Street, New York, NY 10010

Copyright © 2013 by The Rosen Publishing Group, Inc.

All rights reserved. No part of this book may be reproduced in any form without permission in writing from the publisher, except by a reviewer.

First Edition

Editor: Amelie von Zumbusch
Book Design: Kate Laczynski

Photo Credits: Background graphic © iStockphoto.com/Andrea Zanchi; sidebar binoculars © iStockphoto.com/Feng Yu; cover Alan Scheer/Shutterstock.com; p. 4 Leena Robinson/Shutterstock.com; p. 5 Courtesy of Christopher T. Moore; p. 6 Martha Marks/Shutterstock.com; p. 7 Jupiterimages/Photos.com/Thinkstock; p. 8 S.J. Krasemann/Peter Arnold/Getty Images; p. 9 © iStockphoto.com/Peter Burnett; p. 10 Gabriela Hasburn/Aurora/Getty Images; p. 11 Courtesy of Scott Smith; pp. 12, 24, 25 (left) iStockphoto/Thinkstock; p. 13 Cavan Images/The Image Bank/Getty Images; p. 15 Steve Byland/Shutterstock.com; p. 16 © iStockphoto.com/Robin Arnold; p. 17 Slavikbig/Shutterstock.com; p. 19 Shane W Thompson/Shutterstock.com; p. 20 Manuel Montero/Cover/Getty Images; p. 21 (left) cynoclub/Shutterstock.com; p. 21 (right) Olaf Speier/Shutterstock.com; p. 22 Raleigh News & Observer/McClatchy-Tribune/Getty Images; p. 23 Hemera/Thinkstock; p. 25 (right) Jefferson Bernardes/Stringer/AFP/Getty Images; p. 26 Visuals Unlimited, Inc./Robert & Jean Pollock/Getty Images; p. 27 © iStockphoto.com/marmo81; p. 29 Konjushenko Vladimir/Shutterstock.com.

Library of Congress Cataloging-in-Publication Data

Lambert, Hines.
Hunting rabbits / by Hines Lambert. — 1st ed.
p. cm. — (Let's go hunting)
Includes index.
ISBN 978-1-4488-9662-2 (library binding) — ISBN 978-1-4488-9782-7 (pbk.) —
ISBN 978-1-4488-9783-4 (6-pack)
1. Rabbit hunting—Juvenile literature. I. Title.
SK341.R2L36 2013
799.25932—dc23

2012026411

Manufactured in the United States of America

CPSIA Compliance Information: Batch #W13PK2: For Further Information contact Rosen Publishing, New York, New York at 1-800-237-9932

CONTENTS

Good for Beginners

Rabbits like freshly mowed green grass. The edge of a field is a great place to begin looking for rabbits.

Rabbit hunting is a great sport for young hunters. Many excellent hunters began by hunting rabbits. Rabbits are easy to find because they can live almost anywhere! Most hunters return from the woods with several rabbits after a good day's hunt. Many rabbit hunters bring their dogs along when they go hunting.

This makes any hunt more fun. Rabbit meat tastes great, and there are lots of easy ways to prepare it.

Rabbit hunting is good for beginners because it teaches them to walk through the woods quietly. It also teaches them how to hunt alone, with a group of people, or even with dogs. Rabbit hunting is also a good way to learn about firearm safety because your weapon will almost always be pointed down or at the ground.

Rabbit hunting is a great sport both for experienced hunters and those on their very first hunt.

Cottontails and More

There are about 15 **species** of rabbits and hares in North America. There may well be several living close to you! Cottontails are the most hunted rabbits because they are so common. They get their name from their fluffy white tails. There are several kinds of cottontails in North America.

Unlike many other kinds of rabbits, cottontails do not live in **warrens**, or underground tunnel systems.

This is a marsh rabbit. Marsh rabbits are a kind of cottontail.

Snowshoe rabbits are actually hares. They live in cold parts of North America, such as the mountains, Canada, and northern parts of the United States.

Each cottontail digs its own hole. Humans are not the only animals that hunt cottontails. Owls, snakes, and other predators also love to eat them.

Rabbits have developed many ways of fooling predators. Snowshoe rabbits have natural **camouflage**. Their coats change with the seasons! In winter these rabbits' white coats let them blend in with the snow.

Did You Know?

Rabbits and hares look alike, but they have several differences. Hares are bigger and have longer ears. Rabbits and hares are closely related. People use the same methods to hunt both.

Finding and Tracking

Rabbits use camouflage to blend into their surroundings. If you are having trouble spotting them, look for their bright eyes.

The best way to find rabbits is by knowing what they like to eat. If you can find a rabbit's food, you will probably find a rabbit. Rabbits can eat many plants, even poison ivy! Cottontails prefer grass, soybeans, wheat, and just about anything that grows in your garden.

Look for cottontails in open fields, especially ones with woods nearby. They also like heavy brush and bushes.

Rabbits have lots of predators, so they are always looking for a hiding place that is easy to reach.

Following tracks can also lead you to rabbits. Their tracks are unlike those of any other animal. They have two long back legs and two very small front legs. This makes for very strange marks. Tracking rabbits in snow or mud is not hard at all.

Did You Know?

Chasing rabbits is not as easy as it looks. Cottontails can run as fast as 18 miles per hour (29 km/h)!

Rabbit pellets, or droppings, are another clue that there are rabbits in the area.

Laws and Licenses

You must get a hunting **license** before you go rabbit hunting. Each state has different laws for getting licenses. Most states allow you to hunt when you reach the age of 12. You will probably have to pass a test on firearms and hunting safety.

Each state has laws that decide when rabbits are in season. Many allow rabbit hunting only in fall and winter.

It is a good idea to practice your shooting at a shooting range before heading out on your first hunt.

Hunting laws are different from place to place. Research the laws if you plan to hunt in a new area.

Others, such as Arizona, allow rabbit hunting all year. Your state's wildlife office and website will tell you these laws. You can use these sources to figure out the **bag limit**, or how many rabbits you can kill. It is important to follow your state's hunting laws. These laws protect rabbit **populations** for future hunters.

Did You Know?

Some states allow hunters to kill as many jackrabbits as they can. There is no bag limit. Jackrabbits are not really rabbits. They are actually hares.

What to Wear

Smart hunters know how to dress when they hit the woods. Rabbits like to hide in briars and brush. It is a good idea to wear thick clothing and gloves to protect your skin from thorns. Remember, rabbit season often takes place during cold months. You will need to wear warm clothes. Bring along a game bag to carry your rabbits.

The bright orange color that hunters wear is easy to spot, even in bad weather.

Game bags keep your hands free to carry your weapon safely, even after you have bagged your first rabbits.

Some hunting coats have deep pockets that can work as game bags.

Above all, make sure you wear florescent orange. This is a bright orange color that humans can see very easily. Rabbits do not see it very well. Wearing florescent orange will alert other hunters to your presence. It can protect you from getting shot!

Shotguns

There are lots of weapons to choose from, but most rabbit hunters use **shotguns**. When you shoot a shotgun, it scatters hundreds of tiny pellets, called shot. Rabbits run very quickly, but shotguns make it easier to hit these small, moving targets.

Picking the right kind of shotgun is important. Rabbits are not very big, and it does not take a powerful shotgun to kill them. A .20-gauge shotgun is perfect for hunting rabbits. The gauge of a shotgun is determined by the width of the gun's barrel.

Make sure you practice shooting before you go hunting. Good hunters kill rabbits with clean shots. They do not like to leave wounded animals to die slowly and painfully.

Be careful with your shotgun. Never aim at anything unless you are planning to shoot it.

Air Rifles

Shotguns are not the only firearms that can be used for hunting rabbits. Some hunters prefer **air rifles**. These use **compressed** air rather than gunpowder in order to fire. Air rifles do not scatter shot, as shotguns do. Instead, they shoot bullets. They require better aim than shotguns. Unlike shotguns, air rifles have no **recoil**. They are often less expensive to purchase, too.

Air rifles shoot very quietly, so rabbits are less likely to hear a hunter firing one.

Some states do not allow hunting with air rifles, so check your state's website before you take an air rifle into the woods. Air rifles can be deadly, too. Always keep firearm safety in mind. Keep your firearm pointed in a safe direction at all times. Always know where your friends are. Never fire until you are sure of your target.

Practice shooting your air rifle at a shooting range before bringing it along on a rabbit hunt.

Bows and Arrows

Hunting rabbits with bows is difficult but exciting. It is a greater challenge for bow hunters to reach their bag limits. Only the best shots can hit rabbits with arrows.

Recurve bows are popular for hunting rabbits. Their ends curl upward. This makes the arrows fire smoothly and quickly. Other hunters prefer short bows. These are handy since rabbits often hide in thick forests and dense brush.

Most arrows are made from a metal called aluminum. Make sure you choose the right arrowheads. You can ask at a sporting goods store. Since hunting rabbits with bows is such a challenge, it is a good idea to practice. You will need to be an expert shot before you go hunting with a bow!

Hunting with a bow and arrow is known as bow hunting.

A Hunter's Best Friend

Dogs do more than make hunting fun. They can help your hunt be more successful. Some dogs are bred especially for this sport. Most of these are called hounds. They include beagles, bloodhounds, and even miniature dachshunds. Some hunters bring spaniels.

This dog is fetching a rabbit that its owner shot. Finding and bringing back animals that hunters have shot is called retrieving.

Basset hounds were originally bred to hunt rabbits and hares.

This hunter worked with a pointer and a Brittany to catch a hare.

On a rabbit hunt, a dog has two jobs. The first is to smell the rabbit. Most dogs have very strong senses of smell. Your dog's second job is to scare the rabbits out of their cover. Remember, rabbits love to hide in thick bushes and brush. It is a good way to hide from birds and humans, but dogs are closer to the ground. If a dog smells a rabbit in thick cover, it can scare it out for the hunter to shoot.

Beagles

The best rabbit dog is probably the beagle. In fact, beagles are some of the best hunters in the world. A beagle can follow a scent with its nose in the air. It does not have to smell the ground. This lets a beagle run and follow the scent at the same time.

Rabbit hunters often work with packs of beagles. This hunter is preparing one of his beagles for a hunt.

Beagles are known for single-mindedly pursuing a rabbit once they have caught its scent.

When a rabbit is chased, it often circles back to the starting point. Some hunters let their beagles chase rabbits and wait patiently for the rabbits to circle back.

Beagles are not only used for hunting. They are so good at smelling things that they are often trained to find bombs, drugs, and lost people. As many hunting dogs were, they have been bred to be around people. This makes them good pets.

Did You Know?

Beagles use a special bark called "tonguing" to let hunters and other beagles know they are on the scent of a rabbit.

Other Animal Helpers

Ferrets are members of the weasel family. Ferrets are domestic animals, or animals raised by people.

Dogs aren't the only animals used to hunt rabbits. It might sound odd, but ferrets make great hunters, too. Hunters in the United Kingdom have used ferrets to **flush** rabbits out of hiding places that dogs cannot reach for hundreds of years. The hunters release ferrets into rabbits' mazelike underground warrens.

The ferrets search the tunnels and chase rabbits out of them. Hunters wait for rabbits to jump out right in front of them.

Other hunters use large birds of prey called falcons. Falcons can be trained to search for rabbits from the sky. A falcon will dive and kill a rabbit with its talons, or claws. It will then bring the rabbit to the hunter. Believe it or not, there are nearly 4,000 licensed falconers in the United States!

There are more than 50 kinds of falcons. Many wild falcons feed on rabbits.

People who hunt with falcons are known as falconers.

Food, Fur, and Good Luck

If you manage to kill some rabbits, your work is far from over. If you plan to eat your kills, you must **field dress** them as soon as possible. It is a good idea to bring rubber gloves and a clean, sharp knife.

Check for spots when you remove the liver. These are signs that your rabbit may have been sick with

Tularemia is most common in rabbits, hares, and other rodents but can spread to people, too.

Stewing is one of many tasty ways to prepare rabbit meat.

tularemia, or rabbit fever. If you see spots, do not eat the rabbit. Call your state's wildlife office and let them know that sick rabbits are in the area.

Hunters don't just use the meat from rabbits. Some make clothes or hats from rabbit pelts, or fur. Rabbit fur is also used to line the inside of gloves. Other hunters keep rabbit feet for good luck.

Hunters and Habitats

Understand that hunters have responsibilities. Good hunters respect the animals they hunt. Good hunters are also fair hunters. Never shoot a rabbit that is hiding. Wait for it to run out into the open. If you wound a rabbit that is hiding, you might not be able to get it because of the thick brush. The rabbit might suffer as it dies.

Groups such as the Louisiana Rabbit Hunters Association work hard to protect rabbit **habitats**. Being a good hunter means caring for Earth and its creatures. Otherwise, there might be no more rabbits to hunt! When hunters work to take care of the natural world, they make sure that rabbit hunting can be enjoyed for many years to come.

Most rabbit hunters value the natural world and enjoy the time they spend outdoors hunting.

HUNTING TIPS

1 Ask a farmer! Farmers know where cottontails live, and they usually will be happy if you keep the rabbits from eating their plants.

2 Wear an orange hat in addition to a vest or coat. That way, if you are bending down in brush, other hunters can still see your head.

3 In the winter, rabbits often nibble on young trees. Look for young trees when you go on a winter hunt.

4 Early spring is a great time to see rabbits, especially when the grass is beginning to grow. Rabbits are on the move at this time of year.

5 Look for clover! Clover is a rabbit's favorite snack. If you see a large patch, rabbits are likely to be nearby.

6 Go hunting on a snowy day. It is much easier to spot rabbits in the snow. It is easier to track their footprints, too.

7 Try to go out very early in the morning or at the end of the day. This is when rabbits are most active.

8 Remember to look behind you. Rabbits often run away in that direction!

GLOSSARY

air rifles (ER RY-fulz) Guns that use tightly packed air to fire small pellets.

bag limit (BAG LIH-mut) How many of a certain kind of animal a hunter is allowed to kill.

camouflage (KA-muh-flahj) A color or a pattern that matches the surroundings and helps hide something.

compressed (kum-PREST) Squeezed something into a smaller place.

field dress (FEELD DRES) To remove the parts from a kill that would make the meat go bad.

flush (FLUSH) To drive something out from its hiding place.

habitats (HA-buh-tats) The kinds of land where animals or plants naturally live.

license (LY-suns) Official permission to do something.

populations (pop-yoo-LAY-shunz) Groups of animals or people living in the same place.

recoil (REE-koy-ul) The push-back of a gun after it is fired.

shotguns (SHOT-gunz) Guns with smooth insides that are fired from the shoulder.

species (SPEE-sheez) One kind of living thing. All people are one species.

tularemia (too-luh-REE-mee-uh) A sickness found in people, farm animals, rabbits, and other wild rodents.

warrens (WAWR-enz) Groups of connected tunnels.

INDEX

WEBSITES

Due to the changing nature of Internet links, PowerKids Press has developed an online list of websites related to the subject of this book. This site is updated regularly. Please use this link to access the list:
www.powerkidslinks.com/lgh/rabb/